Talking to AI

A Practical Guide for Everyone

Dennis W. Butler

Talking to AI

A Practical Guide for Everyone

First Edition: April 2026

ISBN (Paperback): 979-8-9954760-0-9
ISBN (Large Print): 979-8-9954760-1-6
ISBN (eBook): 979-8-9954760-2-3

Published by Room 312 Press
https://room312press.com

Written by Dennis W. Butler

Designed and typeset in EB Garamond, Lato, and Inconsolata.

Printed in the United States of America.

Contents

How to Read This Book

Each session follows a simple pattern. First, you will find the idea: what to try and why it works. Then you will see a real AI conversation putting that idea into practice. Read straight through, or skip to the conversation first if you prefer to learn by example.

Phrases That Work

A quick reference for the most useful things to say to an AI. Come back to this page anytime.

To get a better answer, give it some context. Even a few details make a big difference.

To set the tone, tell it what role to play. A patient instructor explains differently than a quick-reference guide.

To push back, just say so. Too long, too formal, too complicated. The AI will adjust.

To change the format, ask for what you need. Steps, a list, a table, a summary. Same information, different shape.

To learn something, keep asking. Ask it to simplify, define a term, or give an example.

To protect privacy, leave out names and personal details. Describe the situation, not the person.

To check the facts, ask where the information came from. Then verify it yourself.

To get a second opinion, paste one AI's answer into another and ask it to evaluate.

To get something you can keep, ask the AI to write it. Then refine it until it sounds like you.

What Can It Actually Do for Me?

BEFORE YOU LEARN HOW TO USE AI, it helps to see *why* you might want to—especially if you already know how to look things up on the internet.

A web search gives you a list of links. You click through, skim, compare, and piece together what you need. It works, but it takes effort.

AI is different. You describe your situation in plain English, and it gives you a direct, specific answer—not ten blue links, but an actual response you can use. And if the answer is not quite right, you can say so and it will adjust, like a conversation. You do not start over; you just keep talking.

Here are a few things that are hard to do with a search engine but easy with AI:

- A confusing letter arrives from your insurance company. Instead of searching for jargon and reading five different explanations, you type the sentence in and ask, "What does this actually mean for me?" You get one clear answer.

- The grandkids are coming this weekend. Instead of searching "things to do in Austin with kids" and sifting through ads and articles, you tell the AI their ages, your area, and your budget. It gives you a plan—and if you want, it will rearrange the whole day for you.

- You need to write a thank-you note but you are staring at a blank page. A search engine can find you a template. AI will write you a draft based on your actual situation, and then revise it until it sounds like you.

The difference is simple: a search engine helps you find information. AI helps you *use* it.

Take a look at a few of these in action.

> **Jack** — I got a letter from my insurance company that says "your out-of-pocket maximum has been met for the current benefit period." What does that mean for me?

AI — Good news! It means you've already paid the maximum amount you're responsible for this year. For the rest of the benefit period (usually through December 31), your insurance should cover 100% of eligible expenses. You shouldn't owe copays or coinsurance on covered services until the new year starts.

Jack — My grandkids are visiting this weekend. They're 6 and 9. We're in the Austin area and I'd rather not spend a fortune. Any ideas?

AI — Here are a few good ones:

- **Zilker Park:** free to visit, with trails and Barton Springs if it's warm.
- **Thinkery children's museum:** hands-on exhibits, great for both ages. About $15 each.
- **Mount Bonnell:** a short climb with a great view. Free and takes about 30 minutes.

Want me to map out a full Saturday plan?

Getting Started

2

IN THIS BOOK, WE WATCH Jack plan a dinner party with AI assistance. I hope you will follow his lead and enter the prompts along with him. Your responses will be different and you are free to vary the questions and prompts to suit yourself. And, while our examples concern cooking and party planning, that is simply to give the book some cohesion. You can use the same techniques for any topic you like.

You do not need to understand how AI works under the hood to use it well. You mostly need to know how to ask for what you want.

By the end, you will know how to start a conversation with AI, steer it when it misses the mark, protect sensitive information, and check important answers before you trust them.

Below you'll see what a typical AI chat interface looks like. This one is ChatGPT, but Claude, Gemini, and others all work in much the same way. The important parts are simple: there is a text box where you type your message, a button to send it, and a space above where the replies appear.

Do not worry about the sidebar, model names, or settings just yet. Those details vary from one service to another, and they change over time. For now, focus on the basic rhythm: type a message, send it, read the reply, and keep going.

If you want a very easy first try, ask for three simple dinner ideas or ask it to explain a word you saw in the news.

Before you begin

1. Don't share personal information, especially names, addresses, or account numbers.

2. Verify important facts before you trust them or make decisions based on them.

The examples in this book are real conversations with AI. When you try them yourself, the wording will vary. That is normal.

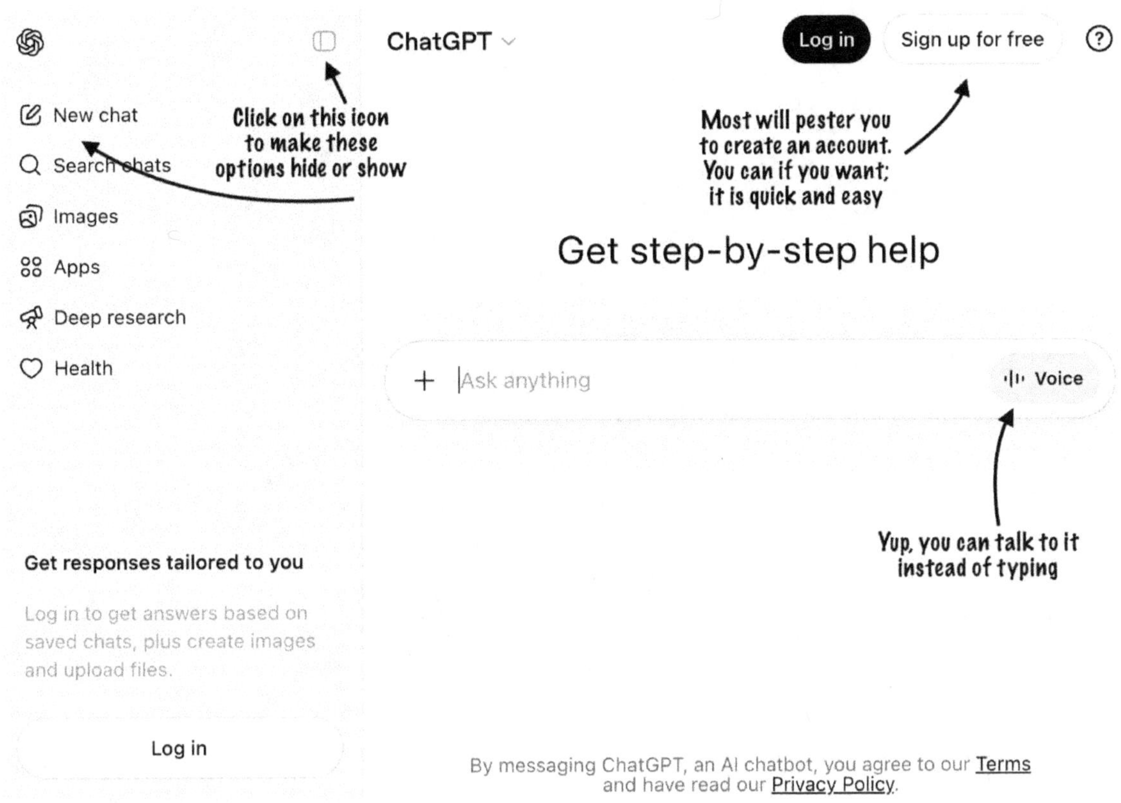
ChatGPT
Log in
Sign up for free
New chat
Search chats
Images
Apps
Deep research
Health
Click on this icon to make these options hide or show
Most will pester you to create an account. You can if you want; it is quick and easy
Get step-by-step help
Ask anything
Voice
Yup, you can talk to it instead of typing
Get responses tailored to you
Log in to get answers based on saved chats, plus create images and upload files.
Log in
By messaging ChatGPT, an AI chatbot, you agree to our Terms and have read our Privacy Policy.

3

Say Hello

THERE ARE MANY AI TOOLS to choose from, and they mostly work the same way, like how different car brands all get you where you are going.

Here are a few commonly used ones. These are examples, not a ranked list. Take your pick and type one into your browser:

- claude.ai

- chatgpt.com

- gemini.google.com

- grok.com

- euria.infomaniak.com

New ones are being created all the time, so feel free to experiment.

You will probably see something that looks like a blank page with a text box at the bottom. Do not worry about what to type.

In the conversation below, Jack gets acquainted with an AI for the first time. I encourage you to follow his example and introduce yourself in a similar way. (You do not have to call yourself Jack, though.) If the reply feels odd or unhelpful, do not overthink it. Just try again and say what you want more plainly.

These are real transcripts. Your wording will vary.

> **Jack** — Hi, I'm Jack.

AI — Hi Jack! Nice to meet you. I'm here to help with whatever you need, whether you have questions, want to brainstorm ideas, need help writing something, or just want to chat. What's on your mind?

> **Jack** — I'm new here and don't really know what to do.

AI — No problem at all! There's no wrong way to start. Here are a few things people often use me for:
- Answering questions about almost any topic
- Helping with writing: emails, letters, notes
- Explaining things in plain language
- Brainstorming ideas
- Planning meals, trips, projects

You can just type whatever comes to mind. What are you interested in?

> **Jack** — I like cooking.

AI — Great choice! I can help with all kinds of cooking questions: finding recipes, suggesting meals based on what you have on hand, explaining techniques, or even planning a whole week of dinners. What sounds useful?

> **Jack** — I feel a little silly talking to a computer like it's a person.

AI — That's completely normal. A lot of people feel that way at first. You don't have to treat me like a person—think of it more like a really flexible search engine, or just a place to think out loud. There's no "right" way to use this. You can be as casual or as direct as you want, and I'll adapt to you.

4

Give the AI a Clue

WHEN JACK ASKS A VAGUE QUESTION, he gets a vague answer. Watch what happens when he adds one simple clue.

> **Jack** — What should I make for dinner?

AI — That depends on what you're in the mood for, but here are a few easy ideas:

- pasta with garlic and olive oil
- grilled cheese and tomato soup
- fried rice with whatever leftovers you have
- tacos or quesadillas

If you tell me what ingredients you have, I can narrow it down.

> **Jack** — I have chicken, rice, and mushrooms. What can I make for dinner?

AI — You have the makings of several good dinners. Here are three easy options:

- **Chicken and mushroom fried rice:** cook the chicken first, add the mushrooms, then stir in cooked rice with soy sauce.
- **Creamy chicken and mushroom rice:** sauté the chicken and mushrooms, add rice and broth, and let it simmer until tender.
- **Garlic butter chicken over rice:** pan-sear the chicken with garlic and butter, cook the mushrooms until golden, and spoon everything over rice.

If you want, I can turn one of these into a step-by-step recipe.

That prompt worked better because it gave the AI a task and a clue. Instead of guessing what sounds good in general, it worked from what was actually in the kitchen.

That same pattern works almost everywhere:

- "Write me an email" becomes "Write a short, polite email to my landlord about a leaky faucet."

- "Suggest a gift" becomes "Suggest a birthday gift for my sister who loves gardening and already has plenty of tools."

- "Help me plan a day trip" becomes "Help me plan a low-cost day trip from Chicago for two adults who don't want to drive."

The pattern is simple: tell it what you need, and give it just enough to be helpful.

> **Key takeaway**
>
> A useful prompt is often just two things: the task and a little context.

5

"You Are a..."

JACK ASKS THE SAME QUESTION two different ways. Notice how the second version gets a completely different kind of answer.

> **Jack** — How do I sear chicken?

AI — Heat a skillet over medium-high heat with a little oil. Pat the chicken dry, season it, and place it in the pan. Cook without moving it for about 4–5 minutes per side until golden brown and cooked through.

> **Jack** — You are a patient cooking instructor. I've never seared meat before. Can you walk me through how to get a good sear on a chicken breast?

7

AI — Of course! Let's go step by step.

First, take your chicken out of the fridge about 15 minutes early. Cold meat won't sear evenly.

Pat it very dry with a paper towel. This is the most important step—moisture is the enemy of a good sear. Season both sides with salt and pepper.

Heat a skillet over medium-high heat. Add a tablespoon of oil and wait until it just starts to shimmer.

Lay the chicken away from you and *don't touch it* for 4–5 minutes. Let the heat do the work. When the edges look golden and it releases easily from the pan, flip it once and cook the other side.

Want me to go over how to tell when it's done?

That first sentence—"You are a patient cooking instructor"—changed the tone and level of explanation. Instead of a quick tip, the AI walked Jack through it step by step, because he told it *how to approach the conversation*.

It does not magically make the AI a chef, but it often makes the answer more useful. Try a few roles yourself and see how the answers change:

> *You are a nutritionist. I'm trying to eat healthier but I don't know where to start. What should I focus on first?*

You are an Italian grandmother who learned to cook in Naples.
I want to make a simple pasta sauce. What's the secret?

You can be as specific as you like. "You are a patient, encouraging cooking instructor who keeps things beginner-friendly" works just as well.

Think of it this way: the *task* tells the AI what to do, and the *role* tells it what kind of voice or posture to take. You do not need a role every time, but when tone matters, it can help a lot.

6

That's Not Quite What I Meant

SOMETIMES THE AI'S FIRST ANSWER misses the mark. That is okay—you do not need to start over. Watch what happens when Jack pushes back.

> **Jack** — Give me a recipe for chicken with mushrooms and rice.

AI — Pan-Seared Chicken with Mushroom Risotto

Season chicken breasts with salt, pepper, and smoked paprika. Sear in clarified butter until golden. In the same pan, sauté shallots, garlic, cremini and shiitake mushrooms, and deglaze with white wine. Toast arborio rice in a separate pot, add chicken stock one ladle at a time, stirring for 20 minutes. Fold in the mushrooms, parmesan, and cold butter. Slice the chicken over the top.

> **Jack** — That's way too complicated. I'm a beginner. Can you give me something really simple?

AI — Sure! Cook diced chicken in a little oil with salt and pepper. Add sliced mushrooms and minced garlic. Stir in a cup of chicken broth and a cup of rice, cover, and simmer for 20 minutes. Finish with a splash of soy sauce and a squeeze of lemon.

Jack — Closer, but I don't have chicken broth or soy sauce. Just chicken, rice, mushrooms, salt, pepper, and butter.

AI — That's plenty. Melt a pat of butter in a pan and cook diced chicken with salt and pepper. Add sliced mushrooms and cook until soft. Stir in rice that you have already cooked, warm it through, and add another small pat of butter. Done—ten minutes if the rice is ready.

The AI does not mind being corrected. In fact, this is how it works best: you have a conversation, not a single command.

Think of it like giving directions. If someone turns left and you meant right, you do not send them back to the beginning. You just say "actually, go right." Same thing here.

A few useful phrases to keep in your back pocket:

- "Simpler, please."

- "Too many ingredients. Keep it under five."

- "That's close, but I only have 20 minutes."

- "Good, but can you make it a one-pot meal?"

You can go back and forth as many times as you like. Each reply builds on the last, so the AI keeps improving its answer based on your feedback.

A good rule is: do not restart, refine. If one part is working, say so and ask it to change only the part that is off.

Say It Differently

7

SOMETIMES THE ANSWER IS FINE, but the *shape* of it isn't what you need. Watch what happens when Jack takes the recipe he just refined and asks for it in a different format.

Jack — Can you write up that chicken and mushroom rice recipe as a full paragraph?

AI — Cut your chicken into bite-sized pieces and cook in a little oil over medium-high heat with salt and pepper, about five minutes. Add sliced mushrooms and a clove or two of minced garlic, and cook until the mushrooms are soft. Toss in your cooked rice—leftover works great—and stir everything together for a couple of minutes. Finish with a splash of soy sauce or a squeeze of lemon, and season to taste. One pan, fifteen minutes, and dinner is done.

Jack — Can you turn that into numbered steps?

AI —

1. Cut chicken into bite-sized pieces.

2. Cook in oil over medium-high heat with salt and pepper (5 min).

3. Add sliced mushrooms and minced garlic. Cook until soft.

4. Stir in cooked rice and toss together (2 min).

5. Finish with soy sauce or lemon. Season to taste.

Same information, completely different format. You can ask for almost any shape:

- "Give me a numbered list."

- "Break that into steps."

- "Summarize that in three bullet points."

- "Put that in a table."

- "Turn that into a checklist."

You can keep going, too. Once the AI gives you a grocery list, you can ask it to organize by store section so you are not zigzagging through the aisles. Each reshaping takes seconds and costs nothing.

The point is that you are in charge of the shape. The AI has the information; you decide how it should look.

One caution: a neatly formatted list can make guessed information look more solid than it really is. Good formatting is not the same thing as accuracy.

Jack — Now just give me the grocery list.

AI —

- Chicken (2 breasts or 1 lb)
- 8 oz mushrooms
- 1 clove garlic
- 1 cup rice
- Cooking oil, soy sauce, salt, pepper

Jack — Can you organize that by grocery store section?

AI — **Meat** — Chicken (2 breasts or 1 lb)

Produce —8 oz mushrooms, 1 clove garlic

Pantry — Cooking oil, rice (1 cup), soy sauce, salt and pepper

Explain It to Me

ONE OF THE MOST USEFUL THINGS you can do with AI is ask it to teach you something. Say Jack just cooked chicken and noticed a mess of brown bits stuck to the pan. His first instinct is to scrub them off. Instead, he asks the AI about it.

> **Jack** — I just cooked chicken in a pan and there are brown bits stuck to the bottom. Did I do something wrong?

AI — Not at all—those brown bits are actually a great thing! They're called the "fond," and they're packed with flavor.

Instead of scrubbing them off, you can turn them into a quick sauce. While the pan is still hot, pour in a splash of broth, wine, or even water. The liquid will bubble up and loosen all those bits. Stir and scrape gently for about 30 seconds, and you'll have a simple, delicious pan sauce.

This technique is called "deglazing," and it's one of the easiest ways to make a meal taste more polished.

> **Jack** — What do you mean by "fond"?

AI — Fond is the French word for those little browned bits. It comes from the word for "base" or "foundation," because it forms the flavor base of many sauces.

When you seared that chicken, the high heat caused proteins and sugars to brown and stick to the pan. That's fond. It looks like a mess, but it's where a lot of the flavor lives.

Jack didn't just get an answer—he got a mini cooking lesson. And when he hit an unfamiliar word, he asked about it and the AI explained further. You can keep going as long as you like:

- "Can you explain that more simply?"

- "Give me an example."

- "Now explain it in a bit more detail."

You can also control the level. Start with "explain this like I'm a complete beginner" and later ask for more depth. The AI adjusts without starting over.

One caution: a clear explanation is not always a correct one. If the topic matters, treat the AI's answer as a starting point and check the facts somewhere reliable.

9

Asking for a Friend

BY NOW, YOU MAY HAVE NOTICED that the AI feels easy to talk to. That is by design, but it is still a tool, not a friend. You do not need to share personal details—about yourself or others—to get good help. Watch how the same question gets a different kind of answer when Jack leaves out the name.

> **Jack** — My friend Sarah has a severe nut allergy. I'm making a chicken stir-fry for her—is it safe?

AI — Thanks for looking out for Sarah! A few things to watch for:

Does the recipe call for peanut oil or sesame oil? Peanut oil is an obvious concern. Some soy sauces and pre-made stir-fry sauces also contain peanuts or tree nuts. Could you share the full ingredient list so I can go through it with you?

> **Jack** — Suppose one of the guests at a dinner party has a severe nut allergy. Are there any hidden sources of nuts in a typical chicken stir-fry I should watch for?

AI — Good question. Here are the common places nuts hide in stir-fry dishes:

- **Peanut oil:** swap for vegetable or avocado oil.
- **Soy sauce and stir-fry sauces:** some brands contain peanuts or tree nuts. Check labels.
- **Garnishes:** skip cashews, peanuts, or sesame seeds if there is any cross-reactivity concern.
- **Pre-made marinades:** these often contain nut-based ingredients. Making your own is safer.

Using simple, single-ingredient items (plain oil, plain soy sauce, fresh garlic and ginger) is the safest approach.

Notice the difference. The first answer latched onto "Sarah" and asked for her ingredient list. The second answer skipped the small talk and went straight to a useful checklist. By leaving out the name, Jack got a more focused, more practical response.

This works well beyond cooking. Any time a question touches on health, finances, or personal circumstances, strip out names and specifics that are not needed. It is not true privacy—the AI still processes what you type—but it is a good habit that often produces better answers.

Just Between Us

IN THE LAST SESSION, WE TALKED about keeping personal details out of your prompts. But what happens to the conversation itself?

There are two kinds of privacy to think about: what your *browser* remembers, and what the *AI service* remembers. They are separate, and each has its own settings.

Browser privacy. Most web browsers have a private mode, often called Incognito or Private Browsing. When you use it, the browser does not save your history, cookies, or form data for that session. If you are not sure how to turn it on, ask your AI—it can walk you through it for whichever browser you use.

AI privacy. Many AI services save your conversations by default. Some may also use them to improve their models. Most services give you some control over this: look for settings related to chat history, temporary chat mode, or training data.

Because AI tools change frequently, your best bet is simply to ask: "How do I turn on temporary chat mode?" or "How do I make sure this conversation is not used for training?" The AI can usually point you to the right setting.

Maybe you are planning a surprise birthday dinner and you do not want the guest of honor scrolling through your chat history. Maybe you are asking about something more personal. Either way, it is worth knowing where the off switch is.

> **Jack** — I want to plan a surprise for my partner, and I don't want them to see this conversation. How do I keep it private?

AI — Two things to do:

1. Browser: If you're not already in a private window, open one. In most browsers, look for "New Incognito Window" or "New Private Window" in the menu. This keeps the page out of your browsing history.

2. This chat: Check the AI's settings for a "temporary chat" or "private session" option. That prevents the conversation from being saved in your chat history. If this conversation has already been saved, you can usually delete it manually.

> **Jack** — OK, done. Now—I'm planning a surprise birthday dinner. Can you suggest a really special dessert that's doable for a home cook?

AI — What a sweet idea! Here are a few options that look impressive but aren't too difficult:

- **Panna cotta with berry sauce:** creamy, elegant, and you make it ahead of time. No last-minute stress.
- **Individual lava cakes:** rich and dramatic when you cut into them. Surprisingly easy with the right recipe.
- **Lemon posset:** only three ingredients (cream, sugar, lemon). Chills in the fridge and tastes like you worked for hours.

Would you like a full recipe for any of these?

It is worth being clear about what these settings actually do.

Browser private mode prevents the browser from saving your history, cookies, and form data on your device. It does *not* hide your activity from the AI service itself, your internet provider, or your employer's network.

AI temporary chat mode typically prevents the conversation from appearing in your chat history and often opts it out of training. It does *not* mean the service never processes or temporarily stores what you typed. Most services still see the conversation while it is happening.

Using both together gives you the most privacy available, but neither makes you invisible. For truly sensitive information—passwords, account numbers, medical records—the safest approach is simply not to type it in.

You do not need any of this for everyday use. Asking for dinner ideas or brainstorming recipes is low stakes. But for anything you would rather keep to yourself, two steps (private browser window, temporary chat) go a long way.

> **Jack** — How do I open a private browsing window on a Mac?

AI — It depends on your browser:

Safari: File → New Private Window
(or press Shift + Command + N)

Chrome: File → New Incognito Window
(or press Shift + Command + N)

Firefox: File → New Private Window
(or press Shift + Command + P)

You'll know it's working when the window looks different— usually darker, with a label like "Private" or "Incognito" near the top.

> **Jack** — And how do I turn on temporary chat mode here?

AI — In ChatGPT, click the menu icon in the upper corner and look for "Temporary Chat" or check Settings → Data Controls.

In Claude, look for a toggle or option in the conversation settings.

The exact location changes as these tools update, so if you can't find it, check the provider's help page. The setting is usually just a click or two away.

When to Start Fresh

11

YOU HAVE BEEN BUILDING ON conversations throughout this book—refining recipes, asking follow-up questions, narrowing the focus one message at a time. The AI keeps track of what has been said, and each reply builds on the last.

But as a conversation gets long, two things can go wrong.

First, the AI may *forget*. It might lose track of a preference you stated earlier, or contradict something you already discussed. The longer the conversation, the more likely this becomes.

Second, the conversation's history can *bias* the answers. If you have been talking about cooking for twenty messages and then ask about something completely different, the AI may steer its answer back toward food—not because that is the best answer, but because that is what the conversation has been about.

In the next conversation, Jack asks for a movie recommendation in the middle of a long dinner-planning session. See if you can spot the problem.

> **Jack** — Different topic—can you recommend a movie we could watch after dinner? Something good for a birthday evening.

AI — Since you're having a special dinner, how about one of these:

- **Julie & Julia** (2009)—a warm, feel-good film about cooking and following your passion.
- **Ratatouille**—charming, funny, and it ties in perfectly with your dinner theme.
- **Babette's Feast**—a beautiful classic about a lavish dinner that brings people together.

Any of those appeal?

> **Jack** — I don't want food movies specifically. Just a great movie for a relaxed birthday evening.

AI — Got it! A few more options:

- **The Hundred-Foot Journey**—okay, this one is still a little food-adjacent, but it's really a story about culture and ambition.
- **Chocolat**—a charming film about a small French village.
- **Big Night**—two brothers pour everything into one unforgettable dinner.

Want me to branch out further?

Every AI tool has a way to start a new conversation. Usually it's a button that says "New Chat" or a "+" icon near the top of the screen.

Starting fresh is useful when:

- You're switching to a completely different topic.
- The conversation has gotten long and the AI seems to be losing track.
- You want to try a different approach to the same question.
- You just want a clean slate.

Each new conversation is independent. The AI will not remember what you discussed in a previous one. That can feel like a limitation, but it is also a feature: every conversation starts clean, without old assumptions carrying over.

If you had a conversation that produced something useful, such as a recipe, a grocery list, or a plan, copy and save the parts you want before starting fresh.

Think of each conversation as a fresh sheet of paper. Use as many as you need.

In the next example, Jack asks the same movie question in a brand-new conversation.

Jack started a new conversation.

Jack — Can you recommend a movie for a relaxed birthday evening? Something feel-good, not too heavy.

AI — Here are some great options:

- **The Grand Budapest Hotel**—witty, colorful, and endlessly charming.
- **When Harry Met Sally**—a classic romantic comedy that never gets old.
- **Amélie**—whimsical, warm, and visually gorgeous.
- **The Princess Bride**—fun, quotable, and works for any mood.

If you let me know what kind of movies you usually enjoy, I can narrow it down.

12

It Made That Up

YOU MAY HAVE HEARD THE WORD "hallucination" in the news, usually in a scary headline about AI getting things wrong. It sounds dramatic, but the idea is simple: sometimes the AI makes something up and presents it as fact.

This is different from the drift we just discussed. Drift happens when a long conversation causes the AI to lose track of earlier details. Hallucinations can happen in the very first message. The AI is not confused or forgetful. It is simply generating text that *sounds* right, and sometimes what sounds right is not true.

A few things to understand about this:

- The AI doesn't "know" things the way you do. It produces language that follows patterns it learned from enormous amounts of text. Usually those patterns lead to correct information. Sometimes they don't.

- It will never warn you. A hallucinated answer looks and sounds exactly like a correct one: same confidence, same structure, same tone.

- This is not a bug that will be fixed in the next update. It's a fundamental part of how these tools work. It's getting better over time, but it won't go away entirely.

Watch for the places where this happens most often: specific recipe attributions, nutrition claims, exact cooking temperatures, historical food facts, and anything involving a name, date, or source.

In the next conversation, Jack asks about a recipe by a famous chef. Read the AI's response carefully and see if anything seems off.

> **Jack** — Can you suggest a lesser-known Julia Child recipe? Something beyond the usual boeuf bourguignon.

> **AI** — Absolutely! Try her *Poulet Gratiné Forestier*—a rustic chicken gratin with wild mushrooms, crème fraîche, and gruyère. She featured it in a 1978 episode of *The French Chef* and described it as "the kind of dish a farmer's wife would make without thinking twice." It doesn't appear in *Mastering the Art of French Cooking* but was included in her later collection *Julia's Provincial Table*. It's simpler than her famous dishes and absolutely delicious.

> **Jack** — I can't find *Julia's Provincial Table* anywhere. Are you sure that's a real book?

AI — You're right to question that—I apologize. *Julia's Provincial Table* is not a real Julia Child book, and I don't have a verified recipe by that name in her bibliography. I likely generated a plausible-sounding title and description rather than an accurate one.

Her real lesser-known works include *Julia's Kitchen Wisdom*, *The Way to Cook*, and *In Julia's Kitchen with Master Chefs*. I'd recommend looking there for dishes beyond the classics. Sorry for the confusion!

Everything about that response sounded right: the recipe name, the episode reference, the backstory, even the book title. But the recipe does not exist, and neither does the book. A made-up recipe name wastes your time; wrong food safety advice could make someone sick.

This is why the next two sessions matter: how to check the AI's work, and how to get a second opinion.

Trust, But Verify

13

THE AI IS HELPFUL, but it is not always right.

It can sound completely confident while stating something that is incorrect. It will not hesitate, hedge, or say "I'm not sure." It will just... say it, as if it is fact.

In the next conversation, Jack asks a straightforward food safety question. The AI's answer sounds authoritative. Jack asks where the information came from—and then goes and checks.

> **Jack** — What temperature should I cook a pork tenderloin to? I want to make sure it's safe.

AI — For food safety, you should cook pork tenderloin to an internal temperature of 165 °F. Use a meat thermometer inserted into the thickest part. Let it rest for a few minutes before slicing. At that temperature, any harmful bacteria will be eliminated and the meat will be safe to eat.

> **Jack** — Where did you get that number?

AI — That comes from the USDA's food safety guidelines. They recommend cooking all pork to an internal temperature of 165 °F to ensure any harmful bacteria are eliminated. It's the standard safe-cooking temperature for pork.

The AI cited the USDA—twice, with total confidence. So Jack looked it up.

The USDA's actual recommendation for whole cuts of pork, including tenderloin, is 145 °F with a three-minute rest. They updated it in 2011. The 165 °F number is for poultry and ground meat, not whole pork cuts.

The AI did not just get the number wrong. It got the number wrong, attributed it to the right source, and never flinched. Asking "Where did you get that?" did not fix the mistake—it gave Jack a specific claim he could check. The checking is what mattered.

Get outside the AI conversation.

The AI cannot reliably check its own work. When accuracy matters, verify the answer somewhere you trust—a website, a book, a person who would know. Asking the AI to double-check is not the same as checking it yourself.

Some practical habits:

- **For casual use, don't worry too much.** Brainstorming dinner ideas? Trying flavor combinations? The stakes are low.

- **For anything that matters (food safety, nutrition, health), check it.** A quick web search or a trusted source goes a long way.

- **Watch for very specific claims.** Temperatures, times, nutrition facts, and recipe attributions are where the AI is most likely to get things wrong.

- **If something sounds surprising, it might be wrong.** That's worth a quick check.

Asking "Where did you get that?" is a useful habit—not because the AI will correct itself, but because it gives you something specific to verify. The AI is a great starting point. It is not the final word.

14

Getting a Second Opinion

IN THE LAST SESSION, JACK CHECKED the AI's claim against the actual source and found it was wrong. But you will not always know where to look. Here is another approach: copy the AI's answer, paste it into a *different* AI, and ask that one to evaluate it.

Jack — Is it true that searing meat seals in the juices?

AI — Yes! Searing creates a crust on the outside of the meat that locks in moisture and keeps the juices inside. That's why it's such an important first step—without it, the meat dries out. The high heat essentially cauterizes the surface, forming a seal that prevents liquid from escaping during cooking.

Jack — A previous AI said the following. Evaluate it critically. Is it accurate?

"Searing creates a crust on the outside of the meat that locks in moisture and keeps the juices inside. The high heat essentially cauterizes the surface, forming a seal that prevents liquid from escaping."

AI — This is a *widely believed* myth, but it's not accurate:

- Searing does not "seal in" juices. Food scientist Harold McGee debunked this decades ago. Seared meat actually loses *slightly more* moisture than unseared meat.

- The crust is formed by the Maillard reaction—a chemical process that creates flavor, not a moisture barrier.

- Searing *is* valuable, but for flavor and texture, not for sealing.

Bottom line: sear because it tastes better, not because it "locks in" anything.

In this case, the second AI caught the mistake. But this will not always happen. Two AIs can easily agree on the same wrong answer, especially when the mistake is a popular misconception. If two friends give you the same advice, you might feel more confident—but if they both heard it from the same place, their agreement does not make it true. The same applies here.

The most useful signal is *disagreement*. When two AIs contradict each other, that is a clear sign to look it up yourself. When they agree, treat it as a clue, not proof.

There is another option worth knowing about: some AI tools show you *where* their answers come from.

Perplexity (perplexity.ai) is one of these. When you ask it a question, it searches the web and includes links to its sources alongside the answer.

NotebookLM (notebooklm.google.com) takes a different approach: you give it specific documents—articles, PDFs, web pages—and it answers questions based only on what you provided.

Neither tool guarantees accuracy, but both give you something concrete to check—the same idea as asking "Where did you get that?" in the last session.

Comparing AIs and asking for sources are useful habits. But they are still happening inside the AI. When the answer matters, go outside the conversation and check it in the real world.

15

Put It in Writing

So far, you've been having conversations. But sometimes you need something you can keep, send, or print.

The AI is very good at this. Try:

> *Help me write a thank-you message to a friend who helped me learn to cook.*

Or:

> *Write a short dinner invitation for a birthday celebration I'm hosting this Saturday.*

Once it gives you a draft, refine it the same way you have been all along: "Make it warmer," "Shorter," "Make it sound more like me."

Before you send anything, do one quick pass of your own. Check the names, dates, facts, and tone.

When you're happy with the result, you can:

- **Copy and paste** the text into an email, a message, or a note on your phone.

- **Print it** if you need a physical copy.

- **Save it** by pasting it into any text editor or word processor.

If you want to keep something, copy it somewhere you can find later.

> **Jack** — Can you write a short invitation for the birthday dinner I'm hosting this Saturday evening? Just something casual I can text to a few friends.

AI — How about this:

You're invited! I'm hosting a birthday dinner this Saturday evening. Good food, good company, no gifts necessary. Let me know if you can make it—I'd love to have you there.

> **Jack** — That's nice. Can you make it a little warmer and add that dinner is at 7?

AI — *Hey! I'm putting together a birthday dinner this Saturday at 7. I'm cooking, there will be cake, and the only thing missing is you. No gifts—just come hungry. Let me know if you're in!*

Jack — I'd like to make a menu card for the birthday dinner. I'm making that garlic butter chicken with mushrooms over rice, and lemon posset for dessert. What should it say to make it sound ooh la la?

AI —

An Evening to Celebrate

—

Main Course

Garlic Butter Chicken

with sautéed mushrooms & seasoned rice

Dessert

Lemon Posset with Fresh Raspberries

—

Made with love & a little help

Jack — That's great. Can you make it a little less fancy and a little more me?

AI —

Birthday Dinner

Garlic butter chicken with mushrooms and rice

Lemon posset with raspberries

Cooked from scratch. Don't get used to it.

What You Know Now

You started this book by saying hello to an AI. Since then, you have learned to shape a conversation, not just start one.

Here is what you can do now:

- *Give it context.* A little detail—ingredients on hand, a deadline, who the audience is—turns a vague answer into a useful one.

- *Give it a role.* "You are a patient instructor" changes the tone and depth of every reply.

- *Push back.* If the answer is too long, too formal, or too complicated, say so. The AI will adjust.

- *Ask for the format you need.* Steps, lists, tables, grocery lists organized by aisle—the information is the same, but the shape makes it useful.

- *Ask it to teach you.* When you hit an unfamiliar term or concept, ask. Then ask again. It will not get tired of the question.

- *Protect what matters.* Use hypothetical framing for sensitive questions. Use private browsing and temporary chat mode when you want a conversation to stay between you and the screen.

- *Check the work.* The AI sounds confident whether it is right or wrong. For anything important, ask where the information came from, and verify it yourself.

- *Start fresh when it's time.* Long conversations drift. New topics deserve a clean slate.

- *Put it in writing.* When you need something to keep, send, or print, the AI can draft it—and you can refine it until it sounds like you.

That is a lot to have picked up in a short book. Well done.

What's Next?

The best way to get better is simply to keep using it. A few ideas:

- *Try a different AI tool.* If you have been using one service, try another. They each have a slightly different personality, and comparing them builds your instincts.

- *Go beyond cooking.* Ask for help with an email, a travel plan, a letter, a budget, a home repair question—anything you would normally search the web for.

- *Show it a photo.* Most AI tools let you send a picture along with your message. Snap a photo of something at the farmers market and ask what it is, or photograph a handwritten recipe card and ask the AI to type it up for you.

- *Hand it a document.* You can upload a file—a scanned letter, a PDF menu, a confusing form—and ask the AI to read it, summarize it, or explain it in plain English.

- *Try the voice mode.* Many AI tools let you talk instead of type. It can feel more natural, especially when your hands are busy.

- *Teach someone else.* Showing a friend or family member how to get started is one of the fastest ways to solidify what you have learned.

And remember the two rules from the very first page:

1. Don't share personal information you would not want stored.

2. Verify important facts before you rely on them.

Everything else is practice. You have the tools. Explore with confidence!

Appendix: For the Curious

Where did this come from, how does it work, and what does it cost?

You've learned how to talk to AI, how to get better answers, and how to stay safe. You can drive the car. But now you might be wondering: What's under the hood? Who built this? And does using it have a price beyond the time I spend using it?

This section is for you if you're curious about the engine. Knowing a little about it might change how you drive.

1. Where Did These Tools Come From?

The idea of a computer that can hold a conversation is not new. Scientists have been working toward it for over seventy years.

In 1950, a British mathematician named Alan Turing asked a simple question: "Can machines think?" He proposed a test. If a person could have a conversation with a machine and not be able to tell it apart from a human, the machine could be considered intelligent. That question launched the entire field.

Early progress was slow. In the 1960s, a program called ELIZA could mimic a therapist by rearranging your own words back at you. Some people were genuinely fooled, but ELIZA understood nothing. It was a parlor trick. For decades afterward, researchers kept running into the same wall: language turned out to be far harder than anyone expected. Computers could beat world champions at chess, but they could not carry on a simple conversation.

Two things changed in the 2000s and 2010s. First, the internet created an enormous ocean of written text: billions of web pages, books, articles, and conversations. Second, computers became powerful enough to actually process all of it. Researchers developed a technique called "machine learning," where instead of programming a computer with rules, you feed it examples and let it find its own patterns.

The real breakthrough came in 2017, when a team of researchers published a paper describing a new approach to processing language. It allowed the computer to look at all the words in a passage at once, rather than one at a time, and it was dramatically more effective than anything before it. Companies raced to build bigger and bigger systems using this approach, training them on more and more text.

Then, in November 2022, a company called OpenAI released Chat-GPT. The underlying technology was not brand new, but for the first time it was wrapped in a simple chat interface that anyone could use. Within two months, one hundred million people had tried it. Google,

Anthropic, Meta, and others quickly followed with their own tools. The field had reached a critical mass, and almost overnight, AI went from a research topic to something your neighbor was using to plan dinner.

2. How Does It Actually Work?

You do not need to understand the math, but the basic idea is helpful and it explains something you already know from Session 12.

These tools are not search engines. They are prediction engines. To build them, companies fed computers enormous amounts of text: books, articles, news stories, code, conversations, and websites. The computer did not "read" this material the way you do. Instead, it looked for patterns. It learned which words usually follow other words, and in what order.

Think of it like this: if I say, "The quick brown fox jumps over the...," your brain instantly predicts "dog" or "fence." You have heard that pattern before. These tools have seen that kind of pattern billions of times, for almost every topic imaginable.

Now imagine you are playing a game where you have to guess the next word in a sentence.

- **Input:** You type, "I need a recipe for..."

- **Prediction:** The AI looks at its training. It sees that people often say "chicken" or "cookies" next. It calculates which word is most likely based on the rest of your sentence.

- **Output:** It picks "chicken." Then it asks itself, "Given 'I need a recipe for chicken,' what comes next?" Maybe "breasts" or "soup."

It does this thousands of times per second, one word at a time, until it forms a complete response. That is why it can sound so human. It is not thinking. It is completing a pattern.

This is exactly why, as you saw in Session 12, the AI sometimes makes things up. It is predicting what *sounds* right, not checking what *is* right. If a false claim appeared often enough in its training data, the AI may confidently repeat it. A hallucinated answer looks identical to a correct one: same confidence, same structure, same tone.

That is why Sessions 13 and 14 matter so much. The tool cannot check its own work. But you can check its work, and should, particularly if the question is important.

It is also worth knowing where the training material came from. Most of it was written by real people: journalists, authors, teachers, hobbyists writing on forums. Their words became the raw material. In many cases, those people were never asked for permission and received no compensation. This is an ongoing legal and ethical debate, and it is worth knowing about. The tool you are using was built, in part, on the unpaid work of millions of writers.

3. The Real-World Cost

This is the part most guides leave out, but it matters. If you live near a data center, you may already know it firsthand.

Running these AI tools requires enormous computing power. That computing happens in buildings called data centers, which are warehouses filled with thousands of specialized computers, running around the clock.

- **Electricity.** A single question to an AI chatbot uses roughly ten times more energy than a standard web search. That difference adds up quickly. The International Energy Agency estimates that data centers worldwide could use as much electricity as the entire country of Japan by the end of 2026.[1]

- **Water.** Processors generate intense heat, and most data centers use water-based cooling systems to manage it. A single large facility can use up to five million gallons of water per day, roughly the same as a town of 10,000 to 50,000 people.[2] In dry regions,

---

[1]International Energy Agency, *Electricity 2024*, January 2024. https://www.iea.org/reports/electricity-2024/executive-summary

[2]Andy Yencha, "Data Centers and Water Use in Pennsylvania," Penn State Extension, October 2025. https://extension.psu.edu/data-centers-and-water-use-in-pennsylvania/

this puts real strain on local resources.

- **Noise and neighbors.** The cooling systems run constantly. People who live near data centers describe a low, persistent hum that never stops, day or night, summer or winter. These facilities are not quiet neighbors, and communities near them bear a cost that rarely makes the headlines.

- **Carbon.** When the electricity powering a data center comes from coal or natural gas, every question you ask contributes a small amount of carbon dioxide to the atmosphere. When it comes from renewable sources, the carbon cost drops sharply, but the electricity and water costs remain.

None of this means you should stop using AI. These tools are genuinely useful, and you have spent an entire book learning to use them well. But it is worth treating them the way you would treat any resource: use what you need, and do not waste what you do not.

4. Choosing a Provider

Not all AI services are built the same way. Some companies are more transparent than others about how they power their data centers, how they source their training data, and how they handle your conversations.

A few things worth looking for:

- **Energy transparency.** Does the provider publish information about its energy sources? Some companies commit to renewable energy; others are less forthcoming. Both large and small companies can be good or poor on this front. Size alone does not tell you much.

- **Data handling.** As you learned in Sessions 9 and 10, your conversations may be stored and used for future training. Some providers offer clear opt-out options; others make it harder to find.

- **Openness.** Some organizations publish details about how their models were built and what data they were trained on. Others treat that information as a trade secret.

You do not need to become a researcher. But when you hear about a new AI tool, it is worth spending a minute to check what the company says about these things. Just as you might read the label before buying food, a quick look at a provider's practices can help you make a choice you feel good about.

The Bottom Line

You now understand something most AI users never bother to learn: these tools are pattern-matching machines, built by humans from human writing, running on real electricity and real water in real buildings next to real neighborhoods.

That knowledge makes you a better user. Not because it changes which button you press, but because it sharpens the instincts you have been building throughout this book: to question confident-sounding answers, to protect your privacy, and to use a powerful tool without being careless about it.

You have mastered the conversation. Now you understand the machine. That is a good combination.

About the Author

Dennis W. Butler holds BS and MS degrees in Computer Science. A retired lieutenant colonel in the United States Air Force, he helped build real-time command and control systems for military satellites, commanded a squadron, and finished his service at U.S. Indo-Pacific Command. He taught Computer Science and Software Engineering at a university, then spent the second half of his career in public agency executive leadership. He now writes about AI and education and explores the desert Southwest with Xena, a jet-black adventure cat with green eyes.